Psychic Stories
Strange
But True

PSYCHIC STORIES STRANGE BUT TRUE

BY LINDA ATKINSON
Illustrated by Marc Cohen

Franklin Watts
New York / London / Toronto / 1979
A Triumph Book

Library of Congress Cataloging in Publication Data
Atkinson, Linda.
Psychic stories strange but true.

(A Triumph book)
Includes index.
SUMMARY: Presents accounts of strange happenings that have been reported by people claiming to have "special" powers. Also includes simple tests to evaluate a person's psychic powers.
1. Psychical research—Juvenile literature. [1. Psychical research. 2. Extrasensory perception] I. Cohen, Marc. II. Title.
BF1031.A85   133.8   79-10259
ISBN 0-531-02861-5

R.L. 2.4 Spache Revised Formula

Text copyright © 1979 by Linda Atkinson
Illustrations © 1979 by Marc Cohen
All rights reserved
Printed in the United States of America
6 5 4

Contents

PSYCHIC!

9

"I Knew What Was in Her Mind"
**THE POWER
OF MENTAL TELEPATHY**

13

"It Was Just Like Being There"
**THE POWER
OF CLAIRVOYANCE**

29

"I Knew It Was Going to Happen"
**THE POWER
OF PRECOGNITION**

41

*"I Looked Back and Saw
My Body Asleep on the Bed"*
**THE PUZZLE OF
OUT-OF-THE-BODY EXPERIENCES**
55

*"I Thought About the Spoon
and Watched It Begin to Bend"*
THE POWER OF PSYCHOKINESIS
65

WHAT DO SCIENTISTS SAY?
77

TESTS YOU CAN DO AT HOME
81

INDEX
93

Psychic Stories Strange But True

PSYCHIC!

Can some people really read minds? Are fortune-tellers actually able to see the future? What about people who know what is happening in places that are far away? Can people really make objects move with just the power of their thoughts? Or leave their bodies and travel thousands of miles in an instant?

People have made claims like these for centuries. Witnesses swear that some of them are true. But are they? *Can* they be?

These people themselves—the "psychics"—can't explain their powers. They talk about "extrasensory perception"—the mysterious ESP. They say it is a special power that belongs to the mind alone. Through it, they can learn about things "directly" without relying on their five senses. They can understand without seeing. They can send messages without sound. They can cause objects to bend and move without ever touching them. Is there such a "mind power"? Is ESP real?

Reports of people with psychic powers come from all over the world. You will read about some of them here. No one is certain of what they mean. Some scientists think all the reports are nonsense.

Others, curious, have begun to investigate. But so far, nothing has been proven.

The reports are shocking. Some are disturbing. And they are all almost—but not quite—beyond belief.

"I Knew What Was in Her Mind"

THE POWER OF MENTAL TELEPATHY

THE CASE OF EDDIE GOULD

It was a Monday morning in November. Eddie Gould, thirteen years old, and his friend Harry Lewis were on their way to school. Suddenly, Eddie stopped dead in his tracks.

"Come on!" Harry called out. "Come on, Eddie! We'll be late!"

Eddie didn't seem to hear.

The cold November wind blew hard and strong.

"What's the matter with you?" Harry called again. Then he reached for his friend's arm.

Eddie turned and ran. He ran all the way home. He was sure his sister Mimi was in trouble. He didn't know how or why. But he was sure.

He found her in the basement. She was huddled on the floor, crying.

"Oh, Eddie," she said between sobs. "I called and called, but no one came."

Mimi, eight years old, should have been on her way to school. But she had stayed behind when her parents left for work. She wanted to feed her kitten.

At the top of the basement stairs, she had tripped. She had tumbled all the way to the bottom. When she tried to get up, her ankle burned with pain. She had begun to cry—and to wish for her brother.

At that moment, Eddie came down the stairs.

THE CASE OF THE MAINE WOODSMAN

The year was 1955. The place, the rural American town of Greenville, Maine. John McCann, a carpenter, was listening to the weather report. He wanted to go to his cabin on Moosehead Lake the next day, but a snow storm was coming. And if it started to snow, he might not be able to get through.

John hoped the storm would pass by. He wanted to spend the whole weekend at his cabin. He loved it at this time of year. And he wanted to see his friend, old Max Steiner. Max was a bit of a hermit. He lived all alone without even a telephone. But over the years, he and John had become as close as brothers.

"Well," John thought, turning off the radio, "if I can't go this weekend, I'll go next."

In the morning, John awoke early. He felt troubled, but did not know why. He dressed quickly and went down to the kitchen. But the troubled feeling stayed with him.

Suddenly, he heard a moan. Then he heard someone call for help. It was his friend Max.

John shook his head. It couldn't be! Max was over a hundred miles (162 km) away! But now the troubled feeling was too strong to ignore. And now John knew what it meant. Max needed help.

John called the police in Moosehead, the town nearest Max's cabin.

"Max Steiner?" the police officer said. "We know him. He lives out on the Lake, doesn't he?"

"Yes," said John. "And I'm sure he's in trouble. Can you get someone out there right away?"

"Max is an old-timer," the officer said. "He can take care of himself. What makes you say he's in trouble?"

John hung up without answering. The police would not understand how he knew. He didn't understand it himself.

He loaded his car with blankets, firewood, and food. Then he set out for Max's cabin.

When he arrived, the old man was asleep. He had a fever of 104° F (40° C).

A doctor said later that if John hadn't come to take care of him, Max Steiner would probably have died.

A CASE OF DROWNING

It was the summer of 1975, and America was suffering one of its worst heat waves ever. Mrs. Stevenson of Wheatley, Arkansas, had to go shopping. But her son Bobby, ten years old, wanted to go swimming in a nearby pond. It was clean and clear, and a safe place to swim. Most of Bobby's friends would be there.

The market was only half a mile (.8 km) down the road from the pond. Mrs. Stevenson dropped Bobby off and drove on. But in the store, she was gripped by a feeling of terror. She could hardly breathe. She felt as though she was choking. Then she realized that it was her son Bobby

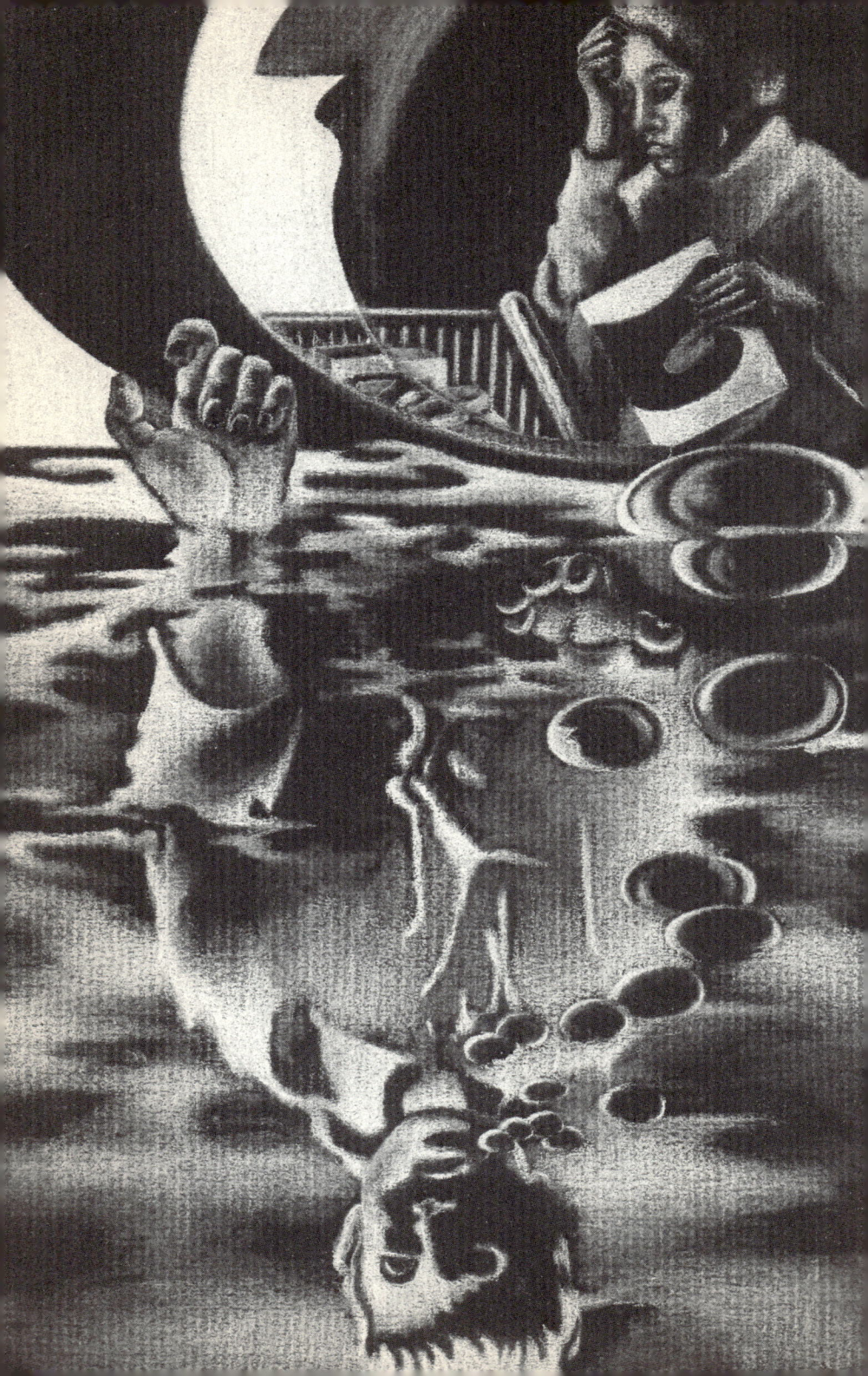

who couldn't breathe. Bobby was choking! He was drowning!

Mrs. Stevenson ran to her car.

"I broke the speed laws and ran through a red light to get there!" she said later.

She did not see Bobby in the water. The other children said they had not seen him for some time.

"I ran to the deep end," she said. "He was lying on the bottom. Two of the older boys dived in and brought him out. He wasn't breathing."

It took several minutes to revive the boy. But Bobby Stevenson lived to tell the story.

Was Mrs. Stevenson's feeling just a coincidence? Maybe.

Was John McCann's?

What about Eddie Gould's?

Perhaps they were all coincidences. But you could never convince the people who experienced them of that. Or the hundreds of other people who have had experiences like theirs. They know something else was involved. They aren't sure just what it is or how it works. But they call it "mental telepathy." Through it, minds can communicate directly with one another.

Eddie, for example, could not hear or see his sister. But when she was hurt and needed help, he sensed it.

"I knew just what was in her mind," he said.

How could he have known? Eddie believes that his mind and his sister's mind made contact through mental telepathy.

Mr. McCann believes that he experienced mental telepathy, too. In some way, his friend's mind sent him a message. And his mind received it.

Mrs. Stevenson is just as sure about her experience. "I can't explain it," she said. "But I knew that Bobby was terrified. I knew he was choking. How did I know? I call it mental telepathy."

Researchers have studied hundreds of cases of mental telepathy. They say that the ones described here are typical. Mental telepathy usually occurs between people who know each other well. Eddie and his sister were very close. So were Mrs. Stevenson and her son. Mr. McCann and Mr. Steiner had been friends for years.

Researchers point out that most cases of telepathy take place between parents and children. Perhaps that is because the tie between them is the closest tie of all. In one case, an Arizona mother received a message from a child who had been missing for years. The boy had vanished at the age of sixteen. The police had searched for him. But they found nothing.

The rest of the family believed that the boy was dead. But his mother did not. She was sure that she would hear from him someday.

After he had been missing for almost four years, she did. She did not learn where he was. But she knew that he was well and that he would return soon.

Two months later, he walked up their driveway.

(As it turned out, the boy had gone over the border to Mexico. There he had been arrested and jailed for carrying drugs. He did not want his family to know, so he had given the police a false name.)

In another case, a young boy knew what was happening to his father, 3,000 miles (4,860 km) away. The boy, David Scribner, was four years old.

He lived in New York City. During World War I, his father was a soldier in France. On November 7, 1917, David was playing in the yard. His mother would always remember the date. It was her twenty-fifth birthday.

Suddenly, David stood up.

"My daddy is choking!" he cried. "He's scared! He's down a hole, and he can't see!"

Mr. Scribner later told his wife what had happened to him on her twenty-fifth birthday. He had been hiding in a cellar. Gas grenades had been thrown inside. He started to choke and thought he was going to die. Finally, his fellow soldiers got him out. But the gas left him blind for three weeks.

Do the cases on record "prove" that mental telepathy exists? No. They are only reports made by ordinary people. They can always be doubted. And they often are.

The people might have been lying, some say. They might have been confused or mistaken. The whole thing might have been a practical joke. Or a coincidence. Strange, perhaps. Disturbing. But still, just a coincidence.

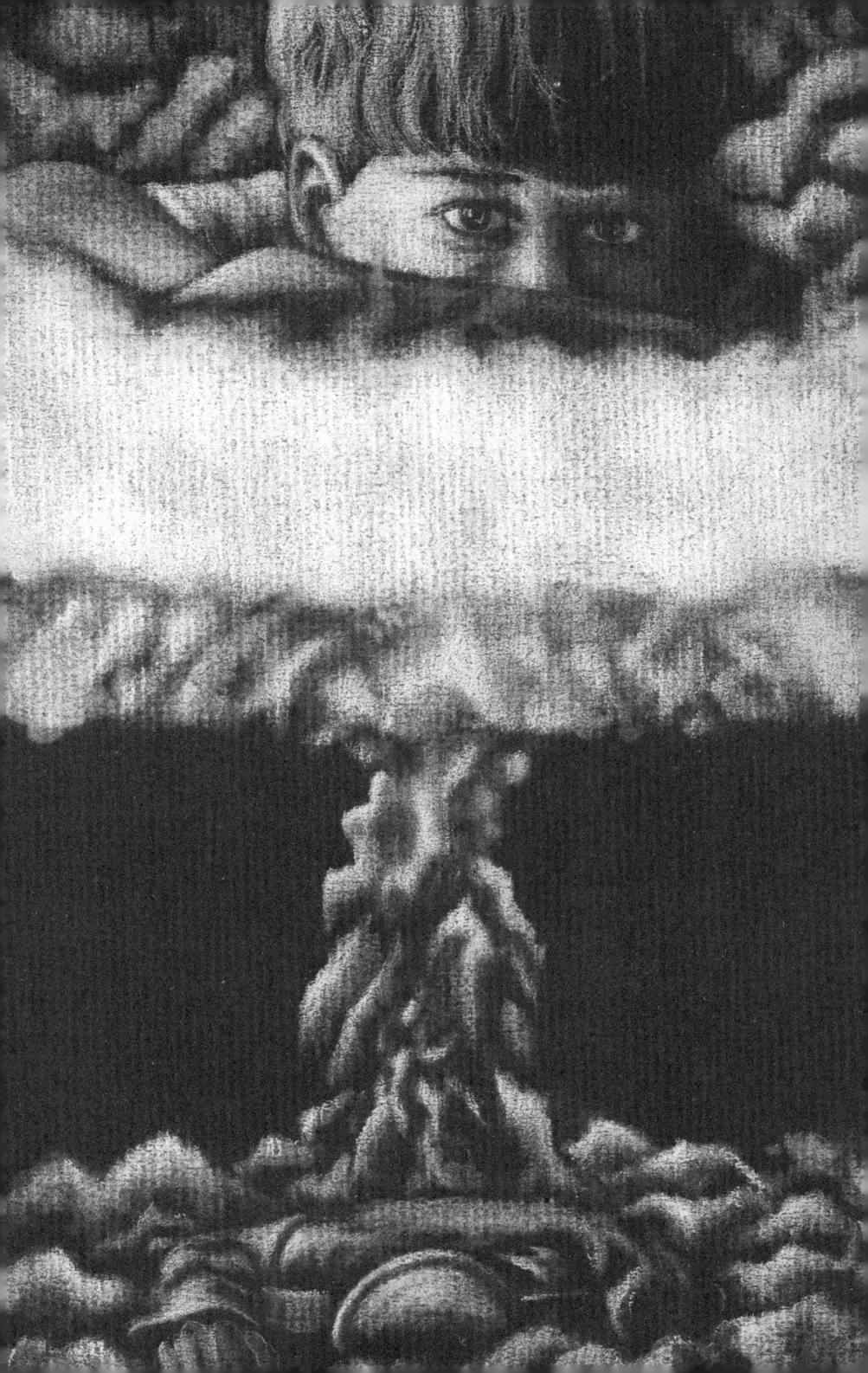

These doubts are easy to understand. Mental telepathy is mysterious. It seems to go against common sense and reason. Most people have to experience it for themselves in order to believe it is real.

Consider what happened to Upton Sinclair, a well-respected journalist of the 1920s. He was known to be a tough-minded man. And he would not take anybody's word for anything. He liked to prove things for himself.

Upton and his wife, Mary Craig, thought the reports they had heard about mental telepathy were very interesting. But they couldn't quite believe them. How could they be sure mental telepathy existed? If it happened to them, they thought, they would know it was real.

Upton and Mary set up their own experiment. It was quite simple. Upton sat in the living room. He drew a picture on a piece of paper. Then he would concentrate on what he had drawn.

Mary, in the bedroom, would close her eyes and relax. Then she would try to imagine the picture her husband had drawn. When she had a clear image in her mind, she would draw it. Then she would call out, "Ready." Upton would come in. They would compare drawings.

The Sinclairs performed this experiment 8 or 9 times a month for 3 years. In all, 290 tries were made. The results were shocking. Of Mary's 290 drawings, only 70 were completely different from her husband's. One hundred and fifty-five were like them in part, and 65 were exactly the same!

Upton Sinclair wrote a book about the experiments. He called it *Mental Radio*. "For the past three years, I have been watching this work day by day and night by night, in our home," he wrote. "Regardless of what anybody can say, there will never again be a doubt in my mind. *I know.*"

"It Was Just Like Being There"

THE POWER OF CLAIRVOYANCE

EYEWITNESS—
AT A DISTANCE

The year was 1759. A party was taking place in a lovely country home in Göteborg, Sweden.

One of the guests was Emanuel Swedenborg. He was a very famous man—a scientist, a philosopher, and a theologian.

When dinner was over, Swedenborg went outside to get some fresh air. When he came back, he was pale.

"There is a terrible fire in Sodermalm!" he cried. "It is out of control!"

The other guests gathered around him. Swedenborg's home was in Sodermalm.

"It began last evening," Swedenborg said. "Many houses have already been burned to the ground. Now the fire is moving toward my home. Dear God, will it be burned, too?"

Swedenborg looked at his friends as though they could give him an answer. Then he turned and went back outside.

For a few minutes, the other guests were silent. What was Swedenborg talking about? He

spoke as though he could *see* the fire. But Sodermalm was 300 miles (486 km) away!

The hours passed. Some of the guests went out to talk to Swedenborg. But he would not answer. He seemed to be in a trance.

Finally, he returned.

"Thank God!" he cried. "The fire is out! It came within three houses of my own!"

The next day, Swedenborg told the governor about the fire. He told him how it had begun. He told him how it had been stopped. He told him what had been destroyed.

Three days later, a messenger arrived. He brought news of the "terrible Sodermalm fire."

It had happened exactly as Swedenborg had described it.

THE MISSING CHILDREN

Joanne and Andrew Tomchik of Burnt Hills, New York, were divorced in the winter of 1972. Every Sunday, Mr. Tomchik came to visit his daughters, aged five and three. One Sunday in April, he took the girls for a drive. He never returned.

Mrs. Tomchik had been afraid that something like this would happen. Her ex-husband had threatened to run off with the children many times. She had even mentioned it to her lawyer. He had told her not to worry about it.

"Lots of men threaten to do that," he said. "But they don't. They just want to upset their ex-wives."

But Andrew Tomchik had really done it.

The police tried to find the children. But there was no trace of them. Mrs. Tomchik hired private detectives. Before long, she spent over $6,000 in fees. Still, there were no clues.

Then, about a year later, Mrs. Tomchik heard about ESP on the radio. She wondered whether a psychic could help her.

She wrote to the group which had sponsored the broadcast. The president of the group told her to get in touch with a Mrs. Millie Coutant. He said that she was their "most gifted member."

Mrs. Coutant studied photographs of the Tomchik children. She put everything else out of her mind and thought only about them. Slowly, a vision came to her. She saw a trailer and a light blue pickup truck. She could not make out the

number on the license plate. But she could see the word "Carolina."

This was more of a lead than Mrs. Tomchik had had in a year of searching. She called the police in both South Carolina and North Carolina. She sent them pictures of the children and of her former husband. She told them she had reason to believe that they were living in a trailer and had the use of a light blue pickup truck.

A month later, Andrew Tomchik and the children were found. They had been living in a trailer park in Wilson County, North Carolina. The light blue pickup truck was found nearby.

How did Millie Coutant find the clue about the Tomchik children?

How did Emanuel Swedenborg "see" a fire that was 300 miles (486 km) away?

Both seem to have had a special mind-power: clairvoyance. That is the ability to "see" things with the mind—things that cannot be seen with the eyes.

How does this power work? Why does it happen? No one knows. But many cases, like the ones reported here, have been sworn to by witnesses. They have had real, practical results. We may not be able to explain them. But we cannot doubt them. They really happened.

The power of clairvoyance is strange. But it is common. In fact, it is one of the most common types of ESP on record.

In many cases, clairvoyance takes the form of a "hunch" or "feeling" rather than a clear picture. Some people ignore the feeling. But others "follow" their hunches. Sometimes, they are very grateful that they did.

Mrs. Lila French, for example, a forty-year-old Pennsylvania woman, did not ignore her hunch. And it saved her husband's life.

Mrs. French had been spending the evening with her parents. Dinner was just over when she had a "feeling" that something was wrong at home. She couldn't explain it. But she couldn't get rid of it either. She called her husband on the telephone. There was no answer.

She decided to go home right away. Her parents thought she was being silly. She felt silly herself. But she just *had* to go home.

When she arrived, she saw flames leaping from the basement window of her house. Her husband was sound asleep on the second floor.

In some cases, a person "sees" something very clearly. But he or she does not know what the picture means. That is what happened to Elizabeth Stoner of Vermont.

Elizabeth and her husband, Steve, were in a restaurant one evening in 1973. Elizabeth was looking out the window while Steve looked at the menu. Suddenly, as she watched, the street lamps outside grew dim. The cars and the buildings seemed to fade away. In place of the street was a winding mountain road. A soft rain was falling.

Then Elizabeth heard the roar of motorcycles. First one, then another, came into view. The first one skidded—but made the turn and kept going. The second motorcycle went out of control. It crashed into the barrier on the side of the road. The body of the young driver was thrown into the air. It came down with a terrible thud.

Elizabeth cried out. As she did, her husband took her hand. And then the scene faded. She was back in the restaurant, safe and sound. The night was calm once again.

The next day, Elizabeth heard some shocking news. Larry Baldwin, a man to whom she had once been engaged, was dead. He had been killed in a motorcycle accident on Mountain View Road. When? At about 7:30 the night before, while Elizabeth was looking out the restaurant window.

In many cases, clairvoyance comes to people in dreams. At the time, the dreamer thinks it is "only" a dream. Later, they learn that what they dreamt about was really happening.

Mrs. Cynthia Barrow had such a dream during World War II. It was about her son David, who was in the navy. Mrs. Barrow woke up screaming.

"I saw his ship," she cried. "It was going down. Davey was hanging onto a life raft. The waves were crashing against him! It was terrible!"

Her husband tried to calm her.

"It was only a dream, dear," he said gently. "Just a dream. It didn't really happen."

The next day, Mrs. Barrow learned that her

son's ship, the U.S.S. *Oregon,* had gone down during the night. Only twelve crew members had made it to a life raft. After five hours in the cold Atlantic, they had been rescued. David Barrow was one of them.

Clairvoyance could be a powerful tool—if it could be controlled. And down through the ages, many people have tried. But no one has ever been able to. For most, clairvoyance is a once-in-a-lifetime experience. Neither Elizabeth Stoner nor Cynthia Barrow ever experienced clairvoyance again. Even people who experience it often—as Emanuel Swedenborg did—cannot depend on it. They can't be sure they will experience clairvoyance, no matter how hard they try.

Clairvoyance seems to be something that *happens* to people, not something they can decide to do. That may be because it has never been well understood. Someday, with more serious study, perhaps it will be.

"I Knew It Was Going to Happen"

THE POWER OF PRECOGNITION

PLANE CRASH IN ALAMEDA

Harry Robinson was the director of the Alameda Hospital in Alameda, California. One night, he dreamt about an airplane crash. He dreamt that it happened nearby.

Robinson was very upset by the dream. He could not ignore it. He could not forget it. When he got to the hospital, he put the staff on emergency alert.

At 2:30 that afternoon, it happened. A navy jet crashed into an apartment house in Alameda. Over a hundred people were hurt. They were rushed to Alameda Hospital. Because of Harry Robinson, the staff was ready to take care of them.

BROTHERS

Sam and Henry were brothers. They lived in St. Louis during the 1850s. They worked on the Mississippi River.

One night, Sam had a terrible dream. He dreamed that Henry was dead. He saw his body clearly. It was in a metal coffin. The coffin was resting on two chairs with flowers nearby. All the flowers were white—except for one red rose in the middle.

Sam woke up. He felt awful. But then he remembered that it had only been a dream. He didn't think about it anymore.

A few days later, Sam and Henry went out on a boat called the *Pennsylvania*. It went down the river to Memphis and then to New Orleans. Henry stayed on the *Pennsylvania* for the return trip to St. Louis. But Sam did not. He signed on a different ship, the *A.T. Lacey*. It left for St. Louis two days after the *Pennsylvania*.

At Greenville, Mississippi, a town south of Memphis, the *Lacey* stopped to pick up supplies. There Sam heard the awful news. The *Pennsylvania* had blown up. Four boilers had exploded when the ship was a few miles below Memphis. A hundred and fifty people had been killed! Many others were hurt. Henry was one of them.

It took the *Lacey* two days to get from Greenville to Memphis. The days seemed like years to Sam. He couldn't stop thinking about his younger brother. He couldn't stop worrying.

When the *Lacey* finally docked, Sam raced to the hospital. There he found Henry. He had been badly burned.

Sam stayed with his brother night and day. At first it looked as though he might pull through. But on the sixth day, he died. Sam, weary and sad, went to a friend's home to rest.

Early in the evening, Sam went to see his brother's body for the last time before it was buried. Things were almost exactly as he had seen them in his terrible dream. Henry's body was in a metal coffin. It was resting on two chairs. And, as Sam stood there, an old woman came in. She went quietly to Henry's coffin and put some flowers on his chest. They were all white—except for one red rose in the middle.

This story became famous, because Sam became one of America's most famous writers. His full name was Samuel Clemens. He signed his books: Mark Twain.

The power to "see" the future is called the power of precognition. It is the ability to know about an event before it happens. In the past, this power was called "prophecy." And most people believed in it. Prophets were thought to be special—and wonderful—people. Kings asked them for advice. Anyone who ignored a prophet was thought to be a fool.

But today, most people find precognition very hard to believe. That is because it is so hard to understand. How can anyone know what will happen in the future? How can they sense something that hasn't happened yet? What is the cause of this kind of experience? Where does it come from?

No one knows. And yet, it seems to happen.

All sorts of people experience precognition. Some have other kinds of ESP, too. But many do not. When they experience precognition, they don't understand what is happening to them. Sometimes, they don't know that what they sense has not yet taken place. The result can be very confusing.

One woman, Pamela Washington, told her husband, Bill, that an old friend had just died.

"I saw Jean Lavonne's death listed in the newspaper," Pamela said. "She had a heart attack. Isn't it awful?"

"But I saw Jean's brother on the train just

this afternoon," Bill said. "He didn't say a word about Jean. You must be wrong."

Pamela tried to remember when she had seen the notice—and where. But she couldn't. She was very puzzled.

Three days later, the notice actually appeared in a local paper. It was the same notice Pamela had already "seen."

In some cases, precognition comes to people in dreams. Sometimes the details are not clear. Sometimes they are wrong. Still, you can tell that precognition was involved. In other cases, many people "sense" the same event. This has happened with a number of well-known disasters. Many people seemed to know they were going to happen.

One of the worst disasters of the century was the sinking of a great ocean liner, the *Titanic*. It was the largest, fastest ship that had ever been built. It was also said to be the safest.

The *Titanic* sank on its first trip. It crashed into an iceberg on the night of April 4, 1912. Fifteen hundred people died.

In the weeks that followed, many people said

they had "known" that something was going to happen to the *Titanic*. Nine sailors had quit their jobs just before the ship sailed. Each of them had felt that it would not make it across the ocean. And at the last minute, seven passengers decided not to sail for the same reason.

Something even more surprising was reported. People who had nothing to do with the ship had felt the same way. By April 1, 1912, nineteen people had said they were sure that "something terrible" was going to happen to it. They had been very frightened by their visions and feelings. Many of them wrote letters to people in the government. Two even wrote to the *Titanic*'s captain. But no one took them seriously.

On October 21, 1966, another terrible disaster happened. Half a million tons of coal waste slid down a mountain in Wales. It had been piled near the coal mines above the village of Aberfan. Two days of heavy rain had turned it into thick, black slush. It was 40 feet (12 m) high when it began to move.

The village of Aberfan was completely buried. Houses and shops were crushed. So was

the schoolhouse in the middle of town. One hundred and sixteen children were trapped inside. They all died. So did twenty-eight adults who were there at the time.

Soon after the disaster, shocking reports began to appear in newspapers. They told of people who had had visions and feelings that "something terrible" was going to happen in Aberfan.

On October 15, a man in a nearby town had told his wife: "Something awful is coming. It's coming soon. And it won't be far from here."

He had visions of coal dust and huge masses of "something black."

On October 17, a woman in London dreamed of children screaming and crying in terror. She saw them trying to escape from a "huge black mass."

On October 19, a London TV producer decided not to put one of his shows on the air. It was a comedy about a mining village in Wales. He had a "feeling" that the show should not go on.

And on the twentieth of October, in the village of Aberfan itself, nine-year-old Eryl Jones told her mother about the dream she had had.

"I dreamed I went to school and there was no school there. Something black had come down all over it."

Then she added that she was not afraid to die.

"Why do you talk of dying?" her mother asked. "You are so young."

"But I'm not afraid, Mother," the girl said. "I shall be with Peter and June."

Peter and June were in Eryl's class at school.

In all, over two hundred predictions were reported in the press after the disaster. They were studied by J. C. Barker, a London doctor. Some of them, he said, did not seem real. They were just "bad feelings" or feelings of fear and worry. Some of them might have been made up after the tragedy happened. But sixty, he said, were real. They did not contain all the details. But they were clear enough. And they had been told to friends or relatives well before October 21.

Could these predictions have helped the people of Aberfan? Dr. Barker thought so. If someone had kept track of them, perhaps the people could have been warned in time.

In 1967, Dr. Barker set up a "tracking bureau" in London. It is called the British Premonitions Registry. In 1968, he helped to set up another group in New York. It is called the Central Premonitions Registry.

"It is time," Dr. Barker wrote, "to stop worrying about *how* precognition takes place. We simply do not know. But while we try to find out, we should keep track of all cases of it. Some of them will be false. But some may be true. Perhaps we can prevent tragedies like the one at Aberfan. At least, we must try."

"I Looked Back and Saw My Body Asleep on the Bed"

THE PUZZLE OF OUT-OF-THE-BODY EXPERIENCES

SYLVAN MULDOON

Sylvan Muldoon, twelve years old, woke up at midnight. He felt as though he was inside a black box. He couldn't see or hear.

He tried to cry out. But he couldn't make a sound.

He tried to get up. But he couldn't move.

Suddenly, Sylvan began to float into the air. Or at least, he *felt* as though he was floating. He closed his eyes tightly and told himself that he was only dreaming. He tried to wake up.

When he opened his eyes, Sylvan could see again. But what he saw frightened him most of all. His bed was far below him. And on his bed, Sylvan could see his own body. It was lying there as if it were fast asleep.

Sylvan rushed out to find his mother. He passed right through the door as he went. When he saw her in the living room, he called to her. But she didn't hear him.

He ran to her and put his arms around her. But she didn't feel him.

Sylvan began to cry.

At that moment, he felt something pull him by the back of the neck. It pulled him back to his room. Soon he was floating above his bed again. He could still see his body there. And it still seemed to be asleep.

Sylvan floated lower and lower. Then he dropped into his body. Everything was still. The next time he opened his eyes, it was morning.

HARVEY REYNOLDS

Harvey Reynolds was a soldier in World War II. On August 3, 1944, his tank was hit by a German antitank gun. The tank blew up. Harvey was thrown 20 feet (6 m) into the air.

He landed in a field. His clothes were on fire, and he screamed in pain. But, he told a friend later, he heard the sounds of his own screaming as though they were coming from someone else.

"I felt," he said, "as though I were two people. One of me was lying in the field. The other was floating in the air. I could see the road and the tank, and I could see myself on the ground. I told

myself to stop screaming. I told myself to roll over and put the flames out."

His body did just that. It rolled over and over. Finally, it rolled into a ditch. The ditch had water in it and put the flames out.

"Then," Harvey said, "I suddenly became one person again."

What can we make of these strange reports? What can we make of people who say they have "floated" out of their bodies? These experiences are called "out-of-body experiences," or OOBE's for short. Are they real? Are such things possible?

It would be easy to dismiss some OOBE's. We can say the people were imagining things. Or dreaming. Some of the people were under a great deal of strain when it happened. Harvey Reynolds was badly hurt and close to death. He may have gone through something truly mysterious. Or, it all could have "happened" only in his mind.

Is that all there is to OOBE's? Maybe.

But some cases are not so simple. Some people have come back with information they did not have before. Others have been seen by witnesses during their travels.

Consider what happened to Mr. and Mrs. Randall Wilmot of Boston, Massachusetts. It may be the strangest OOBE on record. And it has never been explained.

On October 3, 1863, Randall set sail from England for the United States. His wife, Katherine, was at home in Boston.

On the second day, the ship ran into storms. They lasted for six days.

Randall was often sick during this time. He could hardly eat or sleep while the storms lasted. So, on the seventh night, when the sea was calm, he went to sleep very early. And he slept very well. But he had a strange dream.

"Toward morning," he said, "I dreamed that I saw my wife. She came to the door of my cabin. She came to my bed and kissed me. Then she quietly slipped away."

In the morning, when Randall woke up, he found his cabin mate staring at him.

"What was that all about?" the man, William Tait, asked.

"What do you mean?" Randall replied.

"What do I mean?" Mr. Tait smiled. "I mean the woman who was in here last night. I saw the

whole thing. I couldn't sleep, you see, so I was just resting in my bunk. I saw the door open. I saw a young woman come in. She walked over to your bed and kissed you."

"But that is the dream I had," Randall said. "I dreamed my wife came and kissed me! How could you have seen it!"

"I don't think I saw your dream," Mr. Tait said. "And I don't think the woman who was here was your wife."

When Randall Wilmot got home, he was still puzzled. And what his wife said only made things worse. She thought she had visited him while he was at sea!

It happened, Mrs. Wilmot said, one night when she could not fall asleep. At about four o'clock in the morning, it "seemed" to her that she went out to look for her husband. She found his ship and went into his cabin.

"A man was in the upper bunk," she said. "He looked right at me. For a moment I was afraid to go in. But then I went on anyway. I went to the side of your bed. I was so happy to see that you were all right. I kissed you. Then I went away."

What can we make of this case? Did Mrs. Wilmot only dream that she found her husband on a ship at sea? And that his cabin mate was awake? Did Mr. Wilmot just happen to have almost the same dream on the same night? What about Mr. Tait? He saw Mrs. Wilmot. Did he just happen to imagine that he saw her?

These OOBE's, and others like them, cannot be explained. At least, not yet. But many people are studying OOBE's today. One of them is Dr. Charles T. Tart. He is a professor of psychology at the University of California at Davis. He works with people who say they often have OOBE's. He watches them while they sleep. He measures the activities of their brains and sets up tests for them to take.

So far, Dr. Tart has not come up with any answers. But he is still trying. So are other people in the United States and around the world. They believe that someday, they will understand out-of-the-body experiences.

"I Thought About the Spoon and Watched It Begin to Bend"

THE POWER OF PSYCHOKINESIS

THE DISHES THAT CRACKED

Minnie Green and Sara Warren were sisters. They lived in Oakland, California. They were both widows and spent almost every afternoon together.

Most of the time, the women talked about Minnie's son Arthur. He had joined the army in 1950 and was serving in Korea. Minnie wrote to him every day. When she did not hear from him, she worried.

On the afternoon of April 17, 1951, Minnie and Sara were chatting in Minnie's kitchen. Suddenly, Minnie cried out. She pointed at the shelf on the wall.

Sara turned to see what she was pointing at. She turned just in time! The dishes had begun to roll around. Then they broke into pieces. It was as though they were being hit by a hammer.

The women could not believe their eyes.

Had there been an earthquake? They hadn't felt anything. They hadn't heard anything. But what else could have caused the dishes to move and break?

Two days later, Minnie was told that Arthur was in the hospital. He had been badly hurt when his jeep hit a mine—on the seventeenth of April.

BELLS IN THE NIGHT

Mr. Jacques Gerard was very old and very ill. He spent most of his time in bed. When he needed help, he pulled a cord on the wall. That made a bell ring in the hall outside his room. Then the nurse would come.

On the night of August 12, 1836, at 2:00 A.M., the bell began to ring. The nurse went rushing to Mr. Gerard's room. The bell rang out loudly as she went.

When she got there, Mr. Gerard was very pale. He had not pulled the cord, he said. In fact, the bell had woken him up.

The nurse was puzzled. The bell was still ringing. She and Mr. Gerard could see the cord moving up and down. But no one was touching it. No one was even near it.

The next day, a telegram came from Paris.

Mr. Gerard's brother had died during the night. He had died at exactly 2:00 A.M.

In both of these cases, a power called "PK" seems to have been at work. PK is short for psychokinesis. It is the ability of the mind to control objects.

With PK, the mind seems to reach out and "touch" things. Usually, it causes the thing to move. That is what happened in the case of Mr. Gerard's bell. Sometimes, PK causes a thing to bend or break. That is what happened to Minnie Warren's dishes. But always, it is the mind alone that is at work.

For some reason—no one knows why—PK usually takes place at times of death, great danger, and pain. But when it happens at these times, it is very hard to study. It happens suddenly and without warning. People talk about it only after it is over. Some may deny that it happened at all.

Luckily, some people seem to have a special talent for PK. They can use it almost anytime they wish. By studying these people, we have learned a great deal about the powers of the mind.

URI GELLER:
CLOCKS, KEYS, AND SPOONS

Uri Geller is known for his ability to use psychokinesis at will. His story is an important one.

Uri is an Israeli. When he was just a child, he found out that he could make the hands of his watch move. He didn't have to touch them. He only had to wish.

The first time Uri did this, he was in school.

"I just sat there wishing it was twelve o'clock," he said. "When I looked at my watch, it was."

Uri jumped up and started to leave. But no one else in the class moved.

He looked at his teacher. She looked at the clock on the wall. It said 10:30. Uri sat back down. He thought his watch must be broken.

"Stupid thing," he said to his watch. "I wish you would work right."

The hands jumped back to 10:30.

Uri's powers increased as he grew older. By the time he was an adult, he was famous all over Israel. He seemed to have several ESP powers. But PK was the most amazing of them all.

In 1972, Uri was brought to the United States. He spent months at the Stanford Research Institute in California. He was tested by doctors and scientists there, as well as in New York, Baltimore, Seattle, and many other cities. He made spoons and keys bend. He made watches stop. He made them go. Many of the tests were put on film. They were studied over and over again.

Most people were convinced. PK was real—and Uri Geller had it. W. E. Cox, one of the scientists who worked with him, said Geller was "living proof" of PK. Andrew Weil, another scientist, said, "I have no doubt that his PK is real."

But a magician known as The Amazing Randi had something else to say. He said that he could do everything Geller had done. "And so can any good magician," he added.

Randi agreed to perform for the scientists. He made a nail bend. He made a spoon bend. It looked as though he had used PK to do these things. But Randi said PK had nothing to do with it. He had used only magician's tricks. And he thought Geller had done the same thing.

What did Geller have to say about this? He

said that he used magician's tricks, too—sometimes. But only when his powers failed him. Most of the time, he said, they did not fail him. Most of what he did was really done by psychokinesis.

Some people believed Geller. But most people felt that they could not trust him anymore.

Does Geller really have PK? Or is he just a very good magician?

Even scientists still do not agree.

THE SWAMI AND THE NEEDLE

In the 1960s, Americans began to hear stories about a man called Swami Rama from India. People said he could control the beat of his heart. He could control his blood pressure. He could control the temperature of his body. And, he could make things move by the power of his mind alone.

In 1970, Swami Rama came to the United States where he was studied by scientists.

At one meeting, the Swami sat down on a platform in the middle of a small room. A knitting needle was placed 5 feet (1.5 m) away from him. It was attached, through a hole in its middle, to a long metal shaft. The Swami was going to try to make the needle move, using PK.

To make sure that Swami Rama used only PK, a plastic mask was put over his face. A second plastic sheet was placed over his whole body. Only his eyes were left showing.

The Swami was still for a few minutes. Then he nodded his head. He was ready.

The scientists were silent. They stared at the Swami. They stared at the needle. Slowly, it began to move. It moved ten degrees to the right. Then it stopped and slowly began to move back. The Swami had not touched it in any way. No one had. It had moved all by itself.

No one has ever accused the Swami Rama of cheating. No one has ever said that he used tricks of any kind.

Scientists have tried to explain the things the Swami can do. But so far, they have not been able to. The Swami—and a handful of other people around the world—is still a mystery to us. And so is the strange power of psychokinesis.

WHAT DO SCIENTISTS SAY?

Ask three people what they think about extrasensory perception. You will probably get three different answers.

The first person may say, "Yes, I think ESP is real."

The second may say, "I just don't know."

The third may say, "ESP is a lot of nonsense."

Ask three scientists, and you may very well get the same three answers.

Science took its first hard look at ESP almost one hundred years ago. You might think that by now it would have a definite answer. But it doesn't. There is still a lot of doubt and confusion. Why?

For one thing, ESP is very hard to study. Scientists can't just accept the cases that people report. They must see things for themselves. So, they have tried to set up tests that would show ESP in action. But ESP is quite different from the things scientists usually study. And from the beginning, they had trouble setting up good tests.

Some of the earliest ones did not guard very well against cheating. So, no matter what the results, they could not be taken as proof of ESP.

Some tests were not very carefully planned. The results could have come about by pure luck. In others, the results could be explained by something other than ESP.

Many tests seemed fair, but gave results that were confusing. People passed them on one day and failed them the next. They passed when the test was given by a certain person. They failed when it was given by someone else.

All in all, none of the tests was really foolproof. None of them has settled the question once and for all.

And, to make things even worse, fakes were discovered. People lied about what happened to them. They lied about what they felt or did. Even a few scientists cheated. They rigged tests and experiments to get the results they wanted.

Fakes turn up in almost every field from time to time. But in ESP, fakes have been a special problem. The idea of extrasensory perception has always been hard for many people to accept. When one report turns out to be a lie, people wonder about all the other things they have heard. Maybe they were all lies. ESP's reputation suffers. People don't wish to study it. Progress slows down.

Finally, ESP may be ahead of its time. We may not have the tools we need to study it properly. We may not know enough about the brain and how it works. As more is learned, scientists will be better able to deal with ESP. And we may find a scientific answer to the question: Is ESP real?

What can we say then about the scientific case for ESP? It certainly is strong. We have good reason to believe that it exists. But we don't have final proof. Some of us can accept it without that kind of proof. Others may prefer to say, "Let's wait and see."

TESTS YOU CAN DO AT HOME

For all these tests, you need a quiet room to work in. Try to relax. Put everything else out of your mind.

Each test should be done as many times as possible. (Scientists ask people to take them hundreds of times.) But they can be done over a period of weeks or even months. Whenever you get tired or bored, stop. Continue only when you really feel like it.

CLAIRVOYANCE

Black or Red?

What You Need • A complete deck of playing cards (fifty-two in all) • Paper • Pencil

What to Do • Divide a sheet of paper into three columns. At the top of the first column, write "Black or Red." At the top of the second, write "Yes." At the top of the third, write "No."

Shuffle the deck of playing cards. Put it face down on a table. Slide the top card off the deck.

Leave it face down beside the others.

Think about the top card. And think about black and red. What do you think? Is the card black, or is it red?

Take your time. Keep your hand on the card if that seems to help. Just be sure you don't look at the card's face.

When you are ready, write "red" or "black" in the first column on your paper. Then turn the card over. Put a mark in the *Yes* column if you chose correctly. Put a check in the *No* column if you were wrong.

Continue until you have gone through the whole deck.

What the Results Mean • Half the cards in the deck are red. Half are black. So, by chance alone, you should be able to guess correctly half the time. Since there are fifty-two cards in the deck, you should have twenty-six correct calls. If you get more than twenty-six right, something besides chance may be involved. You may be what is called "sensitive." You may have the power of clairvoyance.

TELEPATHY

Card Test

What You Need • A complete deck of playing cards • Paper • Pencil • A friend to help you

What to Do • Divide a sheet of paper into two columns. Call the first column, "The Suit It Was." Call the second column, "The Suit I Called."

Sit down at a table across from your friend. Both of you should be calm and quiet.

Ask your friend to shuffle the deck and place it face down on the table. Then he or she must pick up the first card. You should not be able to see the card's face.

Your friend must look at the card and think about the suit: clubs, diamonds, hearts, or spades. You must focus on what is in your friend's mind. Try to "pick up" the suit he or she is thinking of.

When you are ready, say the name of the suit out loud. Your friend should not tell you whether or not you are right. But he or she should fill out the two columns on the paper.

Continue until you have gone through the whole deck.

What the Results Mean • Every deck is evenly divided into four suits. So, by chance alone, you should be able to name the correct suit once out of every four times you try. Since the whole deck has fifty-two cards, luck alone should lead you to name the right suit thirteen times. If you were right more than thirteen times, you may have been more than lucky. You may have been telepathic.

SINCLAIR DRAWING TEST

What You Need • Several sheets of drawing paper • Two pencils • A friend to help you

What to Do • Give your friend a pencil and three or four sheets of paper. Keep some paper and a pencil for yourself.

Ask your friend to go into another room. You must not be able to see one another.

Your friend must make a drawing. It may be of anything at all—a man, a chair, a cat, a flowerpot. It does not have to be a good drawing. But you should be able to tell what it is.

When the drawing is done, your friend should label it, "Number 1" and call out, "Finished." Then your friend should look at the drawing. He or she should think about it and nothing else.

When you hear your friend say "finished," you must try to sense what he or she drew. Relax. Close your eyes. See if a picture "comes" to you. If it does, draw it. Label it, "Number 1." Then call out, "Ready."

You may stop with one picture if you like. Or you may do more.

When you are finished, call your friend back in. Compare pictures.

What the Results Mean • There is just about no chance of "guessing" what picture your friend drew. So if any of the pictures match, you may well be telepathic. The more times you draw matching pictures, the stronger the case for telepathy.

PRECOGNITION

Card Test

What You Need • 10 playing cards • Paper • Pencil

What to Do • Pick any ten playing cards from a regular deck of cards. Put them face up so you can see them all. On your paper, write down the name of each card. (For example, ace of spades, queen of clubs, and so on.)

Now turn the cards over so you cannot see their faces. Look at the list on your paper. Rewrite the list. Write the cards in the order you think they will be *after they have been shuffled.*

Put your list aside. Shuffle the cards. Then turn them over, one by one. Line them up side by side.

Check the order of the cards against the order in which you listed them on your paper.

What the Results Mean • You have almost no chance of getting the right order by luck alone.

So, if you even come close to the right order, precognition may have been at work.

Keep a Log

Set aside eight or ten pages in an old notebook, or buy a small pad to use as a log. Divide the pages into four columns. At the top of the first column, write, "Today's Date." At the top of the second column, write, "What I Think Will Happen." At the top of the third column, write, "When I Think It Will Happen." At the top of the fourth column, write, "When It Really Happened."

The next time you have a strong feeling that something is going to happen, get your log. Fill out the first three columns.

You may never have anything to write in the fourth column. But if you do, your log will become an important record. If two or three of your predictions come true, you might want to register with the Central Premonitions Registry, Box 482, Times Square Station, New York, New York, 10036. Write to them and ask for more information.

PSYCHOKINESIS

Coin Test

What You Need • Coin • Paper • Pencil

What to Do • Flip the coin into the air or throw it against a wall. While it is falling, think about it. "Order" it, in your mind, to fall on the side you choose. Write down the results of each try. Repeat at least fifty times.

What the Results Mean • The coin has only two sides. So, the chances are 50–50 that it will land on the side you "order" it to land on. Out of fifty tries, luck alone will make it "obey" you twenty-five times. But if you were correct more than twenty-five times, PK is very possibly at work.

When scientists do these tests, they do them again and again—and again. Five hundred times for each would not be too many. You may not be able to do them hundreds of times. But you should do them as many times as you can. The greater the number, the more certain you can be that pure luck is not the only thing at work.

Be sure to keep good records. Make them as complete as possible. There are lots of things you will want to know if your score turns out to be high.

You may want to know how you felt when you took each test. Perhaps you do well only when you are very calm. Or only when you are a little tense. Jot down how you feel just before you begin.

You might also write down the name of the person who helps you. Your ESP may be stronger when you are with some people than when you are with others.

It may be important to note the time of day on which each test was taken. Or what you did just before you took it. Even the weather—rain, snow, sun—might turn out to be interesting.

If you take the tests as many times as you can, and if you keep good records, you may learn some important things about ESP—and about yourself.

Index

Aberfan, Wales, 50–53
Alameda, Calif., 43
Amazing Randi, The, 72

Baldwin, Larry, 39
Barker, J. C., 53–54
Barrow, Cynthia and David, 39–40
Bells, ringing, 68–69
Boating accidents. *See* Ship and boat accidents
British Premonitions Registry, 54
Burnt Hills, N.Y., 32–35

California, University of, at Davis, 64
Card tests,
    clairvoyance, 82–83

    precognition, 88–89
    telepathy, 84–85
Central Premonitions Registry, 54, 89
Children and parents
    and mental telepathy, 23–24
    see also specific incidents, types of ESP
Clairvoyance, 29–40
    test, 82–83
Clemens, Sam and Henry, 43–46
Coal slide, Welsh, 50–53
Coin test, 91
Coutant, Millie, 33–34
Cox, W. E., 72
Craig, Mary, 27–28

Dishes, cracking, 66–67
Drawing test, 86–87; *see also* Sinclair, Upton
Dreams, 39–40, 43–46, 49–53
Drowning, 19–20, 39–40

Explosions, 44–45, 58, 68

Fakes, 79
Families
    and telepathy, 23–24
    see also specific incidents, types of ESP
Fires, 30–32, 38
French, Lila, 36–37

Geller, Uri, 71–73
Gerard, Jacques, 68–69
Göteborg, Sweden, 30–31
Gould, Eddie and Mimi, 15–16, 22
Green, Minnie and Arthur, 66–67
Greenville, Maine, 16–19

Hunches, 36–37

Jones, Eryl, 52–53

Korean War, 66–67

Lacey, (boat), 44–45
Lavonne, Jean, 47–48
Lewis, Harry, 15
Log, keeping, 89
London, 53–54

McCann, John, 16–19, 22
Maine woodsman, 16–19
Mental Radio, 24
Mental telepathy, 13–24
    tests, 84–87
Missing children, 32–35
Mississippi River, 43–46
Moosehead Lake, 16–19
Motorcycle accident, 38–39
Muldoon, Sylvan, 57–58

Needle, moving, 75–76
New York City, 24, 54

Oakland, Calif., 66–67
Oregon, U.S.S., 40
Out-of-the-body experiences, 55–64

Parents and children
    and telepathy, 23–24
    see also specific incidents, types of ESP
Pennsylvania (boat), 44

PK (psychokinesis), 65–76
    test, 91
Plane crash, 43
Precognition, 41–54
    test, 88–89
Prophecy, 47
Psychokinesis, 65–76
    test, 91

Rama, Swami, 75–76
Reynolds, Harvey, 58–60
Robinson, Harry, 43

St. Louis, Mo., 43
Scribner (David's father), 23–24
Scribner, David, 23–24
Sea, accidents at, 39–40, 49–50
Ship and boat accidents, 39–40, 44–45, 49–50
Sinclair, Upton, 27–28
    drawing test adapted for home use, 86–87
Sodermalm, Sweden, 30–31
Stanford Research Institute, 72
Steiner, Max, 16–19
Stevenson, Mrs. (Bobby's mother), 19–21, 22
Stevenson, Bobby, 19–21, 22

Stoner, Elizabeth, 38–39
Sweden, 30–31
Swedenborg, Emanuel, 30–31, 40

Tait, William, 61–64
Tart, Charles T., 64
Telepathy, mental, 13–24
    tests, 84–87
Tests, 78–92
    clairvoyance, 82–83
    precognition, 88–89
    psychokinesis, 91
    telepathy, 84–87
Titanic, 49–50
Tomchik, Joanne and Andrew, 32–35
Twain, Mark (Sam Clemens), 43–46

Wales, 50–53
Warren, Sara, 66
Washington, Pamela and Bill, 47–48
Wheatley, Ark., 19–21
Weil, Andrew, 72
Wilmot, Randall and Katherine, 61–64

World War I, 24
World War II, 39–40, 58–60

LEW WALLACE HIGH SCHOOL LIBRARY

63255

133.8 Atkinson, Linda
ATK
　　Psychic stories
　　　strange but true

DATE			

© THE BAKER & TAYLOR CO